Being happy:
20 tips and exercises for more Happiness in everyday life

Everyone wants to be happy, I guess, but it's not always easy. Especially when the circumstances are unfavorable, we often have the feeling that we can do nothing at all for our happiness. But this is not true, happiness is also or primarily a question of our own thoughts and actions.

Be happy: What's that?
A way to more happiness: Meditation

When are you happy? If you ask different people when they are (or could be) happy, many people tell you about external circumstances: a great job, great love, a nice holiday, a great car, ... Of course, these things can make you happy if you have them. But they are not a prerequisite, and that is a good thing.
Being happy is often a matter of the little things. Many small happy moments add up to great happiness. And you can provide for these small moments, no matter what the circumstances in your life are. We give you 20 ideas, tips and exercises to make you happier.

More luck in everyday life with these tips and exercise

Do things you love

In everyday stress, the things that are actually important to us often get lost. But the thing you love is the best source of happiness. To be happy, you should therefore take time for it regularly. If you do not know what you like to do, it is high time to find out.

Spend time with people who are important to you

Spending a relaxing day with family, sitting with friends, chatting with your old schoolmate... Time with people who are important to us has the best potential for moments of happiness.

Be grateful

Gratitude causes feelings of happiness almost immediately, and the best thing is that we can learn them. As an exercise, you can get into the habit of writing down three things every day for which you are grateful. These can be big, existential things like your children or enough to eat. But even very small moments often leave us gratefully amazed - and happy -.

Reduce stress

Stress is probably the greatest happiness killer of our time. If you just rush from one appointment to another, you have neither an eye for the beautiful things nor time for the things that are important to you. Stress also makes you sick. Enough reasons to reduce stress in your life, right? How to do this is very individual, because it depends on the factors that cause you a lot of stress. Maybe you have to give up tasks; maybe you have to solve open conflicts or even part with certain people. But sometimes it is also rather small things like a better time management or regular short relaxation breaks that help to reduce the stress in your life.

Go outside

Nature is a tremendous source of happiness. This becomes particularly clear when we stand on the beach and look out to sea. But also river banks, forests, flower meadows or snow-covered fields make us happy. And if it's only grey outside: Then at least the daylight and the air do us good. Various studies have shown: that people who are regularly outdoors are also happier.

Learn to say no

Anyone who is constantly being talked into doing tasks (or even goods) is wasting a lot of time, effort and money. Being happy also means knowing what is not good for you and then not doing it if possible. Of course, it is not always possible to avoid that annoying tasks become necessary. But you don't have to say yes to unpleasant diligent work that nobody else wants to do. Learn to say no, and enjoy the small happiness of not having to do an unpleasant task.

Write down moments of happiness

Probably the most effective exercise for more happiness in everyday life is this one: Write down as many moments of happiness as possible every day. Make it a daily habit in the evening and collect at least three happy moments of the day. You may find this difficult at first, but after a short time you will notice that during the day you already pay more attention to what makes you happy. And this leads to significantly more moments of happiness than before.

Do sports

Sport releases endorphins and they make you happy. Exercise also improves our health. And being healthy and fit is also a good basis for happiness. So if you don't do it anyway, you should start exercising more regularly now.

Meditate

In meditation, thoughts can finally come to rest and make room for relaxation. Many people therefore find meditation a great factor of happiness. Just give it a try.

Care for a balance between giving and
Taking

Those who are constantly only concerned with their own advantage will not be happy in the long run. The one who constantly only gives and empowers himself in the process will not be happy either. Really happy are those people who on the one hand can accept good things, but on the other hand are happy to pass them on to others. This can refer to many areas of life: money, time, compliments, attention, help...

Treat yourself lovingly

Let's be honest: How do you actually deal with yourself? Do you respect your needs? Do you encourage yourself in your thoughts or do you make yourself rather small when something doesn't work out? Do you make sure that you get everything you need for your well-being? Many people have the impression that other people are responsible for such things, but this is a big mistake that quickly makes you unhappy. First and foremost it is up to you to treat yourself with love.

Banish things (and people) that harm you

What's not good for you? What tasks, objects or even people are you constantly annoyed about, without there being any good times? If there are such factors in your life, you should seriously try to get rid of them. Nothing and nobody has the right to harm us permanently. Ban such things and also people from your life.

Ensure a good sleep

We all know from experience that sufficient sleep is an important factor for happiness. Yet we often do far too little for it. There are many ways to ensure better sleep: going to bed early. Relax in the evening. Optimize the bed and bedroom so that they provide real resting places. Adjust the daily schedule to your own biorhythm as much as possible. Do without alcohol. What is your problem with sleeping badly? And how can you change this?

Find beauty in your surroundings

A little exercise that you can do anytime and anywhere: No matter where you are, try to find something beautiful in your surroundings. Even a tiny little thing is enough to make you look at the positive and become happier.

Live in the here and now

You cannot change the past and how the future will develop, you cannot foresee today. Happy are especially those people who manage to live a lot in the here and now. This means not constantly dealing with the past and not seeking happiness in an uncertain future. If you want to be happy, then be happy now, no matter what the circumstances are.

Learn to forgive

Old anger and hurt feelings can be real happiness killers. The cure for that: Pardon. Many people do not want to or cannot forgive because they are not clear about one thing: your grudge doesn't hurt the person who hurt you, only you. The other person usually doesn't notice much of it, but you yourself have to deal with the bad mood again and again. Forgiving does not mean forgetting everything or condoning a deed. It only means to free you from the injuries of the past.

Look at what you have

Many people pay particular attention to the things or abilities they would like to have but do not have. The neighbors have a bigger car, the girlfriend is slimmer and actually the man for life is still missing ... If you constantly focus your thoughts on the lack, it makes you unhappy. Turn your attention to the things you already have. Because they are the basis for your happiness. You can practice this view with the gratitude exercise that we have introduced to you above.

Smile

A few years ago, something amazing was discovered: The brain seems to get information from the facial muscles about how we're doing. This means that when you smile - even if you don't feel like smiling - you are signaling to yourself that you are fine, and the brain is releasing the appropriate messenger substances that actually make you happier. Smiling at yourself and others can make you happy for that reason alone.

Start today

Shifting your happiness into the future doesn't work. If you want to get happier, you have to start today. Just choose two or three of the tips you like best and put them into practice today.

Thank you for choosing my book, please write me a review if you liked this book, it's very important to me, because it's hard to become known as a new author and every review would help me. Thank you for your time you sacrifice for me.

These remaining pages are for you to write down what you have done for your happiness today, and if it has brought you any closer to being a happy person!

28

33

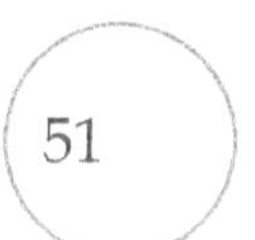

51

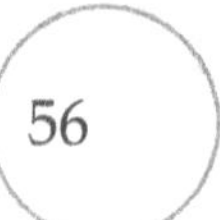

72

You're walking the right way

77

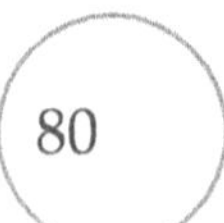
80

99

108

111

118